The Tracings Of My Shadow

ISBN-13: 978-1725894990
ISBN-10: 1725894998

Introduction

The Tracings Of My Shadow

I look behind your gone.

I look ahead your gone.

Story of my days here on earth,

how much emotion are you worth.

Tracing thoughts following their path

in my mind,

memories of every kind.

Taking time to read this book,

all the shadows that it took.

The traces of a smile linger here and there.

Tears leave streaks whilst falling everywhere.

This book is about musings past,

of things and times that never last.

Experiences of life and youth.

Told with love and with truth.

Some of the poems are of me and others of thee.

There's also one about the beginnings of a tree.

Some of them about my life, and some of other's woes and strife.

Laughter they say is good for you.

So, for good measure we have those too.

Please enjoy this book.

Part One: Various Musings

He Rode the Sea

Well-practiced he stood his ground as the waves swelled and broke the sides,

this courageous young man who braved the elements and high tides.

He shivered with the cold which seeped through to his core.

A hundred odd miles off the shore.

Nets cast... far over the side

trawling an area a few miles wide.

Rain and wind beat relentlessly down as he stands without fear,

a smile on a face weatherworn and old beyond its years.

Perhaps he missed his step, or a wave carried him away.

We can only guess what happened to him on that day.

Another brave soul shields his eyes, as he holds on tightly and looks over the side,

to be greeted by a face staring back at him eyes opened wide.

Resigned to his fate, he waves a farewell as he slowly descends,

to a man with whom he had always been friends.

A lone figure in headscarf and coat,

stands patiently waiting on the shore for his boat.

Heavy with child, she is young and unsure.

She stares out to sea anxious and afraid,

playing out a scene which has often been played.

With no family to help no guiding hand.

She stood alone. When she could stand.

A bottle for company to help her forget,

her former life which she could never regret.

Her love never returned he was lost to the sea.

Another fatherless child left calling *Why me, why me.*

She wanders the shore every now and then,

in the vein hope she might see him again.

An Acorn's Story

Long ago my mother tree, grew an acorn, that was me.

I fell onto the dusty ground where I just rolled round and round.

A hungry squirrel had her eye on me,

a juicy little morsel for her tea.

She approached with the intention of wolfing me down.

Until a bigger squirrel came along, eyebrows raised with a deadly frown.

In the hubbub and kerfuffle, I rolled right under some rubble.

Dark and warm between those bricks,

just the place I would have picked.

I sent my root to explore the soil, to anchor me firmly in place,

where the squirrel cannot find me, I haven't left a trace.

Through the winter I rest and sleep, drinking every now and then.

As spring creeps across the forest floor, I find myself awake again.

My shell makes an awful sound as it cracks and falls onto the ground.

I stretch young shoots to find some light, to feed me from the warm sunlight.

Beginnings of a tree that is me.

As long as those pesky birds leave me be.

I have been left alone, and a few years on I have grown.

Next to me stands a mighty oak tree, if I am lucky that

could be me.

The seasons gently come and go, woodland plants putting on show after show.

One winters day as I slumbered, I felt a hand softly stroke my bark.

One man points and calls to another, 'This one would look grand in the park!!'

I am dug around and ripped up from the ground.

From that safe place which I had found.

I am shaking and rumbling along in a truck.

Discarding roots and plenty of muck.

Finally, we come to rest, and wait for it, this part is the best.

Carried gently to my new home, lowered carefully into a pre-dug hole.

From where they had recently evicted an angry mole.

Space and light abound, in this new home that I have found.

This is just the place for me.

It is where I will become a mighty oak tree.

Hope Ain't Gonna Float

Sadness drapes your shoulders like a well-worn coat.

Feet dragging heavily no hope to float.

An empty house once full of laughter and light.

Welcomed you home as you returned each night.

Now darkness greets you as you reach that door.

No more light, no warmth any more.

The aroma of cooking once such a normality.

Lacking in your life is now your reality.

Slumped in your chair you stare at the blank screen.

So many nights held in your arms, her favourite movies seen.

A microwave dinner. Milk before bed.

You lay staring at the pillow were she once laid her head.

A tear trickles silently before you drift away.

Praying that you won't have to greet another day.

The dawn arrives quickly, too quickly for you.

Family arrive, all chatter and try to cheer you on.

You smile but inside you want to be gone.

As you wave and smile you close the door.

No hope to float here anymore.

Whisky glass in hand you drift into slumber.

A dream of days past too many to number.

You wake with a start to be greeted by the dark.

To a silence so deafening you cover your ears.

Then cover your eyes now flowing with tears.

You dance all alone to her favourite tune.

Swaying slowly to the light of the moon.

Your whiskey glass sits empty alone on the bar.

One final goodbye one final hurrah.

No more lonely nights filled with endless sorrow.

For you my dear friend there will be no tomorrow.

For Ged

A Hot Evening in August

Dew drops sit atop the grass.

Waiting for the clouds to pass.

Evaporating into to the air.

As I recline in my chair.

Vines hang heavy with their fruit.

Waiting to be robbed of their loot.

Languorously I observe the passing of the day.

An avenue of trees in full leaf as they sway.

Sipping leisurely from a frosted glass.

Wishing this moment would never pass.

Reflecting on the fleeting quality of time,

as I sit and sip my wine.

Your furtive glances even now.

The unbidden but welcome raising of a brow.

Gently as the day flows on.

Dew drops replaced by a searing sun.

The song of the Cicada becomes a deafening hum.

The passing river charts it's inevitable course.

Ever onwards no remorse.

A Gallic Rooster proudly mounted on the entrance gate.

His owner's presence he patiently awaits.

As the birds all take flight.

The evening softly welcoming the night.

A cool breeze gently caresses my skin.

Silken sheets to wrap myself in.

Drifting slowly into a restful slumber.

Did I ever get that guys number?

Solitude

There sits a silent room in the middle of a house.

Where you can hear the stirrings of a visiting mouse.

A room in which to contemplate.

With logs burning in the grate.

Devoid of all technology.

A solitary room for me.

A leather sofa sitting proud.

Favourite poems read out loud.

Books line all four walls.

Where the darkness casts shadows as evening falls.

Enfolding me in its warm embrace.

The trials of life briefly erased.

Wait for me little room.

I will be there very soon.

Wandering

I sit and wander through my thoughts.

So elusive but waiting to be caught.

I hover above the page, white and crisp as it beckons my pen.

Like the scalpel to a patient it waits to descend.

Wisps of smoke appear and fade before my plans can be solidly laid.

Fingers run through unruly hair, as I sit in my chair.

The more I chase, the more they race.

Those thoughts to which I try to hold, become torture to recall.

It simply drives me up the wall.

Walking my dogs in the park, my brain cells decide to spark.

There you are... stay right here, elusive thoughts don't disappear.

Panic ensues as it becomes quite clear they are gone again I fear.

Tangled in a mass of leads searching for a pen or phone,

I twist this way and that searching as I groan.

People ask do I need help as the dogs begin to yelp.

I smile and thank them politely I'm sure they think me mad.

I can't tell them I am searching for some thoughts I just had.

There is Beauty

They made a handsome couple,

both modest and unaware.

I would go further there was beauty there.

Pulling and heaving her way up through life.

A wonderful mother and caring wife.

Working hard living life to the full.

I can honestly say it was never dull.

Life can be ugly the things we do ugly too.

I saw in them a beauty the ugliness could not erase.

A beauty which life would never fade.

He boxed in the army and skied in Trieste.

After having his appendix out.

He put his yoga skills to the test.

Beauty is not worn like a dress or suit.

You cannot play it like a harp or flute.

It cannot be put on or taken off.

Beauty you do not wear.

Beauty is just there.

Man Is The Beast

You pass me every day sat far back in my cage.

Soft liquid eyes weary tired resolute.

There was a time long ago, I was called cute.

You see me, but you don't see me at all.

Your feet drag heavily as you try not to fall,

bucket clattering the bars as you pass.

It's nearly my time.

Perhaps if I close my eyes turn to the wall you will pass me by forget I exist.

Because if you don't forget... tomorrow I will no longer be,

not even a memory.

Her Heart

They stood

picking

like a dog at a bone

tearing it to shreds ripping it apart.

She stood

watching

It had been her home

her heart.

The Feather

Just hiding behind my eyes.

Those tears I work hard to disguise.

I want to scream cry howl shout,

"Don't take me out,

let me stay, this is my forever home,

my forever place, my heart place."

I know we have to go... I know,

so, I just cannot let it show.

Its ripping the guts out of this frail tired body.

Leaving all, leaving my heart.

Where will I be, what will I be when we part.

I am a feather blown this way and that by life.

All I wanted was to be your lover your wife.

Lying beside me oblivious sleeping.

While inside I am weeping.

"What are you doing?" you ask briefly awake.

"Writing." I feel more than hear you moan.

I am lost alone.

Just a feather waiting to be blown.

One Night

Awake in my bed,

animals tucked up and warm in their shed.

The rain beating a persistent drum, soft splatters on the glass.

We wait patiently for the storm to pass.

The gate begins to loudly rattle,

as the elements go into battle.

Lightening illuminates the sky,

the crash of a bolt from on high.

A branch torn cruelly from its tree.

Lashing rain making it impossible to see.

The claps of the applauding thunder,

as it watches on in wonder.

Wind howls and rips at every dead and living thing.

Delighted to see the devastation that it brings.

I lay wrapped in his arms, ears closed to the sounds,

as the rain and wind whip the ground.

Shuddering windows rattling glass.

I pray it will soon pass.

I sense a change... a retreating of the combatants.

Battle lines erased. Withdrawing from the chase.

Slowly peace returns to the land,

as we remain hand in hand.

Fearful of the scene we will face,

we drift into sleeps comforting embrace.

One of those days

There it was one of those days she sat down to have a cup of tea.

It had appeared from outer space to knock that smile off her face.

Her mind keeps pondering as it keeps wandering.

Deep and dark unbidden thoughts like a river meander through her mind.

Memories not always kind.

As she paces her mind begins to race,

memories you wipe that smile right off her face.

Distraction her own reaction.

Lead on dog a trip to the bog.

Let's get out, hurry out,

to find a place where she can scream and shout.

A lone figure with a dog on a lead,

sat on a bench in a park listening to the singing of the lark.

People hurry by,

trying not to catch her eye.

The mist finally begins to clear,

she asks, "What am I doing here,

sat in my nightgown,

wearing nothing else other than a frown?"

I Remember

I remember your swathe of thick black hair,
and how you strode everywhere.

I remember the deep timbre of your voice,
and how you made us laugh we had no choice.

I remember the wisdom of your words,
and how you loved to be heard.

I remember your fingers were tapered and long
and how your hands were so strong.

I remember how you smoked your cigarettes,
and you often liked to have a bet.

I remember you never read a book
and could never understand my need to look.

I remember how you would come home late
and how mother would sit up and wait.

I remember the stories that you told,
and how we thought you would never grow old.

Most of all...

I remember being your child.

The Huntress

The huntress stalks as she walks,
her instincts sharp and honed.
She no longer wants to be alone.

The huntress does not do menial work.
No stacking shelves,
or washing dishes for someone else.
She doesn't want to work nine to five just to exist and stay alive.

Instead of spending hours in front of a mirror
she could be designing some haute couture.
Not for our huntress all that stress.
She doesn't do work or mess.

If you meet and fall in love that's ok,
you will live to fight another day.
If you hunt him down to put in a cage,
I am afraid your mistake is grave.

The huntress is not only you,
there are others on the prowl who will catch him too.
Beware those smiles that beguile,
for he will no longer be yours in a while.

Softly is the best approach

genuine feelings do not need to be coached.

Love and desire which pierce the heart,

will seal a bond almost impossible to part.

Love is blind to wrinkles and age.

Together you turn each and every page.

Do not fear that the huntress may be near.

You can fell her in one, with your spear.

Cooking up a Storm

The pot is warm, brimming with love.
The moon is high shining brightly above.
Our love is a delicious meal,
to be savoured and eaten with zeal.

The ingredients too many to list,
a touch of lust to give the odd twist.
Each course adding to the fun,
now that the night has just begun.

Our table is laid out for a feast,
four courses at the very least.
The touch of your fingertips on my arm,
I never could resist your charm.

Transported by our passion,
a love never going out of fashion.
A meal for two consumed with joy,
emotions not played with like a toy.

The table now laid to waste,
tracings of a smile play on your face.
The pot is empty but still warm,
after all we did cook up a storm.

Part Two: The Masks We Wear

Mask

The show I put on is just for show.

The glow I wear is just a glow.

A shine so fragile it may break.

The frosted mirror.

Opaque.

Mortality

Last night a shadow came to me.

Linked arms and took me on a journey.

It took me to places I didn't want to go.

It whispered things I didn't want to know.

A soft pillow brushing my arm.

Its smothering presence had me alarmed.

Shadow why do you want me?

Are there secrets you want me to see?

We walk side by side.

There is nowhere I can hide.

I shake my arm.

Trying to brush you off, but still you remain.

My step faltering, as your shape you keep altering.

Perhaps you will go as you came.

I hope... but I doubt.

I know nothing will ever be the same.

We walk together now.

Mighty Warrior

Don't hide from me,

you are inside.

I caught a glimpse of you.

You came to me mighty warrior you conquered all my fears.

I can feel you now, I know that you are near.

I am sat in the dentist's chair of life.

A smile struggles to stay with me.

Fear crouches on weak shoulders.

You like to hear the mighty roar of your voice.

Reveal yourself.

I need you.

You are me.

Sitting

I sit waiting for you.

Stillness holds me prisoner.

My body held fast.

Surely this madness cannot last.

Seconds pass by.

Each one stretches out before me.

A tunnel into which I stare.

I feel a presence are you there?

A raging torrent swirls inside.

The ebbing and flowing of the tide.

Invisible chains bind me.

Chains nobody else can see.

Silence little voice inside my head.

Soon he will be asleep in bed.

If he doesn't notice me.

Perhaps it will still his misery.

We tried we failed, it was too much.

I flinch at the slightest touch.

Living with someone who wasn't you.

There was nothing else I could do.

I had to save us all.

To say goodbye, to leave the past.

The memories stay locked inside.

Something from which I cannot hide.

Staying strong is the key.

It saved both you and me.

Remote Control

Independence has always been my goal.

Still you remain my remote control.

A machine is all I have ever been.

Switch me off a blackened screen.

Forget

The sun beats down on your head,

as you lay still upon your bed.

A silken sheet of purple hue,

covers the identity of you.

Curled inside that silken chrysalis,

emerging limbs unfold and stretch.

Wings unfurl put to the test.

No place to hide anymore.

A door opened by another door.

Show your face, you have changed.

Wipe your memory it can be arranged.

Your beauty can no longer be hidden.

That horse of life has to be ridden.

© 2018 Taylor Crowshaw

Whispers

How easily those words trip from your tongue.

Softly spoken still they are wrong.

Like poison delivered from a viper's bite.

Swiftly gone as in the dead of night.

Sickly murmurings soft as silk.

Still the words drip drip from your cup of milk.

Oh, how easily you sigh.

You hear my breath catch as you wander by.

Thick and heavy your words rain down.

Their smothering voice in which I drown.

You are blind, can you not see,

those whisperings destroying me.

I am bowed, defeated, the battle lost.

I surrender.

My life the cost.

Stuck in A Room

A life spent stuck in a room,

static oppressed filled with gloom.

Shhh!! no noise, no distress,

they cannot deal with all that mess.

A fist clenched inside my chest,

mind telling me to rest.

Tiptoeing around you day and night,

no resistance no will to fight.

So many are trapped inside those rooms,

hoping to taste some freedom soon.

© 2018 Taylor Crowshaw

Smile

Where are you behind that smile,

I have not seen you in a while.

Your hollow laughter I can hear,

I know you must be somewhere near.

I want to reach in and pull you out,

if I do you will only shout.

Retreating again to your safe place,

with just a smile on your face.

The Book

A book, the book, is somewhere to hide.

It gives relief from the pain inside.

Another world which exists only in our minds.

Reality of another kind.

You can go there but not travel at all.

An escape from within your walls.

The dark shadows of the dawn.

When hope seems lost and dreams forlorn.

A book lays beside my bed.

I will travel there in my head.

Finally sleep arrives.

The book has helped me to survive.

© 2018 Taylor Crowshaw

Hope

Fluttering inside this breast.
Wings beat slowly before they rest.

A future unfolds in my mind's eye.
Chance to live if I dare to try.

I stumble I fall I look behind.
Into a past where hope does not dwell.
Where my dreams do not end well.

Those fluttering wings again I find.
The past is left far behind.
Dreams awoken hope dawning.
Curtains pulled back on a new morning.

Fly High

There was a time when I could fly.

Wings of dreams soaring high.

Goals and futures holding promise.

Breath held, pushing onwards

Each bring their own rewards.

The peace age brings is not lost on me.

The pleasures of a simple cup of tea.

Reflecting on times past.

A time which could never last.

My dreams still carry me on.

Optimism has never gone.

Those goals may not be the same,

but my hope in them still remains.

My cup is half full.

Personality never dull.

I still dream, I still fly.

No matter how many years have gone by.

I Will

Didn't you say it would be all right.

Before you tried to hold me tight.

You said it would be okay,

but then you tried to run away.

Why can I not shake that memory.

What use is it now to me?

We torture ourselves with hows and whys.

Not even knowing the reasons why.

So often when we look back.

Diverting ourselves from the right track,

but forge ahead my little voice said.

Hard to do in the loneliness of my bed.

In a while I won't look back.

My life adjusted back on track.

Why do we do this to ourselves?

Put our lives under a microscope.

It never helps us to cope.

But I will.

Your Bed

While you lie in your bed,

I cry tears in the shed.

The torrent which I cannot stem,

glistening like jewels upon my hem.

Children's breaths softly exhaled,

unaware of my love which failed.

Sleep your sleep of ignorance my little ones.

When morning dawns my memory of it will be gone.

Now that we have grown old,

you are no longer cold.

My touch brings comfort not distress.

All your needs I can address.

No longer do my demands overwhelm.

Fingers entwine beneath those sheets.

A pleasure when our bodies meet.

The impetuosity of youth.

A relief when gone this is my truth.

Chained to the fire inside,

I am released no more need to hide.

I am now beside you in your bed,

no longer crying in the shed.

A life shared put to the test.

Bed a place not of misery but of rest.

Joy

Joy transcends this mundane life.

Catching the wind and taking flight.

No explanation for the feeling in my breast.

This fluttering within my chest.

I know there is more I can achieve.

Giving me the space the breath.

Inhaling deep the crisp clean air.

My joy bursts forth I am aware.

Beauty unfolds before my eyes.

When I reach for the sky.

Grasping that illusive dream.

I know I can hold it in my fist in my heart.

We cannot be prized apart.

Do not try to take from me.

The feeling of when one becomes we.

I can move forward with hope and joy.

It is my life not a toy.

Tick Tock

The silence booms.

Inside my room.

Silence hangs as it looms.

In the stillness and the gloom.

It's comfort and rest from craziness.

Relaxing I feel I am blessed.

Until I feel refreshed again.

When the silence begins to irritate my brain.

Boom boom in my room.

Boom boom in my head.

That ticking clock beside my bed.

The silence deafens me.

The clock threatens me.

Time ticks relentlessly by.

Why do I feel more alone?

When the clock begins to groan.

I cannot bear the deafening sound.

Those incessant clock hands ticking around.

Reminding me of days past.

Of the fact that nothing ever lasts.

Faces of the people I recall.

The vastness of life makes me feel small.

Take the clock from my room.

Open the curtains eliminate the gloom.

Fill the space with light and sound,

and stop those hands from spinning around.

The Dress

The dress hangs alone behind the door.

It cannot be worn anymore.

Ripped to shreds in your jealous rage.

Your paranoia I could not assuage.

An innocent glance.

A misplaced smile.

Your jealousy they would rile.

Green and white dress my only one.

Now destroyed, now you're gone.

You were a symbol of my youth.

Independence lost in truth.

We didn't last for very long.

To treat me that way was so wrong.

Goodbye young love you disappeared.

To be replaced by loss and fear.

Although a lifetime has now passed.

I find those memories still last.

A recording playing in my head.

While trying to think of pleasantries instead.

Strength

You have strength if you dig deep down inside.

Do not be afraid, do not hide.

Look into the palm of your hand.

Your future is there at your command.

Only you have choice.

Do not let them take your voice.

Crush the want crush the fear.

Your salvation is so very near.

Open the door and walk through.

You know what you have to do.

Leave the past far behind.

Live a life of another kind.

Do not be bound by invisible chains.

Break them take control again.

I know it's hard I've been there too.

You hold the cards it's up to you.

Run from it while you can.

Do not deny what's going on.

Just be honest and get gone.

Throw your baggage in the bin.

This is a battle you can win.

They are all waiting on the other side.

The ones who love you will be at your side.

Do not let pride dictate your fate.

Your future is there it cannot wait.

Look at me I am free.

I have lived a life.

You can be me.

Ripped Away

You came to see me for a day
departing too soon ripped away.
The wall I had built over time tumbled and fell.
I had to stay when you crossed the sea
you have others... dad only has me.

Siblings raised along with me,
loved but lost across the sea.

A mother so loved but so far away,
appears now and then just to be ripped away.
An emptiness replaces emotion.
Loneliness replacing your devotion.

Stomach wrenching gut churning tears as I lay,
you are always ripped away.
I want you to give comfort a place to rest,
to soothe this aching in my breast.

I want to beg you to stay,
but I still my voice, my tears, as I smile and wave.
You have taken so much from me.
Every time I want... I need you to stay.
Yet again you're ripped away.

Look

Look! It's him, have you heard?
They're looking for him and he's running scared.

Charging around in his three-wheeler car.
Chug chug he won't get very far.

Whisper whisper he beats his wife.
Whisper whisper he's not very nice.

There're children too did you not know.
Perhaps it's better that he goes.

It was an accident, so they say.
He hasn't always been that way.

Blue lights flashing here we go.
Let's settle down and watch the show.

You Held Me With Your Tears

You played to all my fears,
you held me with your tears.
I'm trying to hold on,
even though all love has gone.

You bound me in your chains,
your love drove me insane
I tried to leave again.

You held me with your tears.

A moment in my life,
I held you as my wife
it wasn't meant to be
I'm trying to break free.

I caught your reflected smile,
still crying all the while.
You played me like a harp.
You broke my weary heart.

You held me with your tears.

Our child used like a weapon.
The isolation that you threaten.
Pulling my invisible cord,
while screaming that you're bored.

My feelings have all gone,

I just can't carry on.

I'm running on a wheel.

My pain I can't conceal.

I try to keep it real.

The misery I feel.

I beg you let me be,

why can you not see

I just want to be free.

Don't hold me with your tears.

Overwhelmed

Clenched into a ball,

this life into which I fall.

A tsunami of emotion

rises like a wave on the ocean.

Sick of life of all this strife.

Sick of selfishness it's such a mess.

Sick of pain.

Sick of feeling sick of sick.

Tears so many to shed.

Head in hands in my bed.

Deep exhalations of breath,

how long until death?

No future in my eyes,

sadness I cannot hide.

So much sorrow in the world,

hard to bear for a simple girl.

Where will it end?

The sun will still rise again,

children will be born, laughter and joy will be heard.

The cogs still turn the workings of this world.

No point in trying to hide.

I have no choice but to stay until the end of this ride.

Pull down the shutters on all the strife,

try to live my life.

© 2018 Taylor Crowshaw

Wall Of Silence

That fortress you built and sit inside.

The place in which you choose to hide.

Walls that took years to build,

a love which your silence killed.

I feel like a book on your shelf.

You pick me up and read me for a while,

then close the pages with a smile.

File me neatly away to be picked back up another day.

I am a compartment of your life sometimes a mother, a lover or a wife.

Just as I thought it was too late,

when I had made plans to vacate.

You came from behind your walls you lowered the gate.

Knowing I would no longer wait.

I can't decide If I am being played,

or if it was the right decision that I made,

when I put my plans away and stayed.

Those bricks, that wall which tumbled down,

will you build it back up again?

One by one will those bricks steal my time,

or will you finally draw a line?

Part Three: Try The Fridge

When Did My Mother Arrive

Looking in the mirror through bleary eyes.

I asked myself, "When did my mother arrive?"

I hear her voice calling my children *'love'*.

Blimey, when did my mother arrive?

A reflection in a window, an expression on my face.

Crikey, when did my mother arrive?

My mother arrived with her smile, my smile.

My mother arrived when I became her child.

Where Are You

Where are you, sexy beast?

Where are you, sultry siren?

Where is all that power?

Have you deserted me in my midnight hour?

You have left me behind.

To live a life of another kind.

No more the chase.

Life's endless race.

Time marches at a slower pace.

My lovers' body,

a map familiar and well-travelled.

Roads crossed and recrossed.

Each line a testament to our time.

Perhaps that siren still lies deep inside.

Waiting for the moment to arise.

I Have Become My Daughter's Daughter

"Oh, mother that skirt is far too short,

and do you really need to drink that port?

When will you be back? Oh, by the way it's cold, don't forget

your hat."

"Please do you have to sing?

I'm trying to give my friends a ring.

You're playing that music far too loud.

Do you want to attract a crowd?"

"I think that colour is too bright.

Perhaps you could wear something a little lighter."

"Don't you think that neckline is a little low?

Perhaps it would be better if you didn't go."

"YES MUM." I respond as I grab my coat and run along.

Try The Fridge

"Have you seen my phone?"

"Try the fridge" my children groan.

"Where did I put that sugar?"

"Why don't you try the fridge mother"

"Where are my glasses?"

"On your head" my children said, "but you could try the fridge instead."

Please do not be deluded.

Not every item is included.

Sometimes the things that I misplace,

disappear without a trace.

© 2018 Taylor Crowshaw

My Feet Have Gone Missing

The last time I looked down,

I'm sure I saw them on the ground.

When I was sitting in my chair,

I'm quite sure that they were there.

I couldn't see my brand new shoes.

I couldn't see my slippers,

and even though they were big, I couldn't see my flippers.

In the end what I found,

when I was looking to the ground.

If I slightly adjusted my belly.

Finally, I could see my wellies.

© 2018 Taylor Crowshaw

The Greys

When the greys first appeared,

And then increased year on year.

There was nothing I could do.

Along came the lines too.

Shout out

They are mine!

I have lived!

I am alive!

I survived!

Jill

Oh, Jill, you funny old dog,
you just had to go into the bog.
You rolled around in the mud,
getting as dirty as you possibly could.

Oh, Jill that twinkle in your eye,
how those years have hurried by.

Now...

The wall you leapt is just a wall.
The ball you chased now just a ball.

Twitching limbs as you sleep.
Dreams of some far-off beach.

Faithful Jill enjoy your slumber.
Age is really only a number.

Life

Nature is wonderful, good food is a treat.

The company of our loved ones makes us complete.

Our children are a precious gift but there is no need to hurry.

For along with them comes a lifetime of worry.

We raise them with a guiding hand,

and pray that they understand.

Trying to avoid our parents' mistakes.

Swearing we will never be the same,

life is like a complex game.

We make mistakes of our own, different

ones for sure.

Nevertheless, they are mistakes, we realise...when we become mature.

Life is a journey on the road to our end.

We can make it straight, or with many a bend.

It can be lonely and difficult sometimes.

If we let our eyes wander up into the sky.

We will find joy and wonder with our teary eyes.

The magic of a pale blue sky with cotton wool clouds drifting by.

A tree in full leaf, a coat of green makes it complete.

The vastness of the deep blue sea,

brings a stillness inside of me.

A world of wonder lays elsewhere,

For us all to see and share.

Not everyone wants to go.

That's fine too they should know.

What can compare to the greeting of a furry friend.

Asking for nothing other than their needs to tend.

They worship us with all their heart...

and never want from us to part.

A critical eye they do not possess.

When they look upon our dress.

To our wrinkles they are blind.

Beauty to them is of a different kind.

Hair Today

The hair so thick when we were young.

Sometimes disappears or grows where it does not belong.

Once a chap came to our house.

My daughter said, "Where is your hair?"

He pointed to his chest and said, "It slipped down there."

The colour fades, as we age.

Another turn of another page.

Accept it or don't.

It is your choice.

It doesn't mean we have to lose our voice.

There is no place to hide

Life sweeps us along on the tide.

Time has made us interesting.

If only they would listen.

A wealth of knowledge to draw from.

Before that day when we are gone.

Let's Have A Cup of Tea

"Aunty Ethel's here."

"Let's have a cup of tea!"

"Mum I've grazed my knee."

"Sit down lad. You better have a cup of tea."

"Dad, I am marrying Tim."

"Mother! Put some whisky in that tea!"

"Uncle Henrys gone!"

"Well you better put the kettle on."

"Mary's having triplets!"

"Give dad a shout, and put that blooming kettle back on."

© 2018 Taylor Crowshaw

Quick, The Sun's Come Out

"Quick, the sun's come out."
" Get your shorts on", mum did shout.

We can't bring ourselves to take them off.
Although our neighbours often scoff.
Sunbathing in-between the clouds.
Playing music very loud.

Barbeques primed and ready.
The drone of the mowers as they keep their course steady.
"Get those chairs out our lass, but don't you mess up my grass!"
"Freddie get those bats, and the rest of you put on your hats!"

The first few drops begin to fall, as I give my kids a call.
"It's going to pour down!" I say with a frown.
"Get inside before you drown."

Bed Beckons

A child does not want its bed,

it would rather do anything instead.

When I was younger I could sleep all day,

as I grew older that urge went away.

The painless sleep my bed provides,

brings a tear to my eye.

Instead of staying up until three,

I find that my bed beckons me.

Click Click

Out of bed I stretch and yawn.

As the stiffness of my back begins to dawn.

Click click, as my shoulder settles in.

My waiting socks seem to grin.

Elastic snaps me back as I try to bend.

Frustration boils as my needs I tend.

The time it takes me to rise and dress.

Frustrates me greatly I confess.

Once I finally start to get going.

I can do most things even the mowing.

Do not write me off yet.

I still have strength do not forget.

It may take me a while to go,

but look at me I can still mow.

The Path We Tread

Tangled bodies dream as one.

Still hope and longing has not gone.

Comfort and warmth from each other.

There will never be another.

A scent familiar and evocative.

Memories brilliant and provocative.

Skin to skin our love began.

For all those years it ran and ran.

Time is cruel harsh and rough.

We have grown strong and tough.

A love so deep and ingrained.

A friendship nurtured and retained.

A knowing smile, a touch, a laugh.

Both treading the same path.

We may not reach the end together.

But enduring love lasts forever.

The Guest

You came to me when I was not there.

Sitting beside me in my chair.

I turned to you but could not see.

My eyes closed to save me.

I stand and face the mirror stroking my face.

Where is that young woman? There is no trace.

As I smile I can see the creases and lines.

Each one betraying my time.

Empowered full of energy and strong.

I never noticed things starting to go wrong.

Slowly you arrived I did not notice you there.

Until you sat beside me in my chair.

© 2018 Taylor Crowshaw

Who Said That?

Someone once said to me.
You need to write amazing poetry.

I can only write the words that come into my head,
but I would love to write amazing poetry instead.

Is there a special formula of which I am unaware?
Or do they pluck the words from out of thin air?

The words appear to me as if I'm being fed,
but I would just love to write amazing poetry instead.

I feel as if I'm always clowning around.
Looking everywhere for amazing poems to be found.

I can't find them anywhere, even under my bed.
So, I'll just have to write whatever pops into my head.

Mum's Dancing Finger

When I dared to give cheek.
My mother would wag her finger at me.

If I refused to make her tea.
My mother would wag her finger at me.

If I came home late, I would see,
that finger wagging in front of me.

I would find myself mesmerised,
as she wagged that finger before my eyes.
I thought, 'If she does that one more time,
I will have to cross the line.'

I found my teeth begin to crunch.
When I imagined that finger as I munched.
Of course, that situation did not arise,
but I still see that finger dancing before my eyes.

Bath Night

Bath night in those days,

was different in so many ways.

No bath bombs at that time.

Just bath cubes and I can't make that rhyme.

Not enough hot water for everyone.

Mother would always say, "Once it's gone it's gone!"

First one and then another.

Please don't let me be after my brother.

Mum roll on if we were lucky,

and a nearly clean towel if we weren't too mucky.

It was such a bind.

All the muck that was left behind.

That is why the last one out, always gave a shout.

They had to clean up the mess, before they could even dress.

A Mouse Tale

We once sat together on the bedroom floor.
Watching out in case anyone came through the door.

The table tipped upside down and made into a boat.
If we imagined hard enough, we were sure it would float.

Out of the corner of my eye.
I could see a tiny mouse... skipping by.

We gave a little shriek and the mouse disappeared,
but we could always sense that he was near.

Never did we tell anyone about that little mouse.
For all I know he could still be skipping around the house.

A Box Of Buttons

When I was a child.

I was not wild.

Trying to create magic.

My efforts were usually tragic.

Until I saw the treasure.

A box of buttons and a tape measure.

Oh, such things I would create.

With some fabric and that tape.

Self-taught, nothing bought.

Imagination and images caught.

Those skills have served me well.

Look at my clothes, can't you tell.

Breathless

The depleted quality of the air.
Not enough oxygen for two to share.
A scorching heat intense in its ferocity.
Leaves me questioning my impetuosity.

A Valencian sun beats down on me.
No shade to find no bowing tree.
Trickling sweat on my brow.
Release me from this tortuous heat NOW

I imagined myself wafting in a perfumed haze.
That my beauty would amaze.
Drinking wine and eating tapas.
Now none of that frippery matters.

I trudge along ten paces behind.
My energy levels are low I find.
Instead of strolling hand in hand.
We look like players in a marching band.

A holiday meant to be such fun.
If I had a choice from it, I would run.
Instead of looking like a Greek goddess,
I just look like a bloody mess.

Nanna is a Yodeller

My nanna she could yodel it was her special turn,
When she went out for a drink to yodel she would yearn.

She never travelled very far,
only to where she could reach by car.

The Alps was far out of her reach,
her yodelling for to teach.
Instead she went up to the school,
to teach them yodelling as a tool.

The local sheep just stood and stared,
when at first the yodelling they heard.
Soon enough they understood.
That they should move as quickly as they could.

At the agricultural college,
they decided to increase their knowledge.
Off to Switzerland they all flew,
so that they could learn to yodel too.

© 2018 Taylor Crowshaw

Taylor Crowshaw

Born in Fleetwood, Lancashire,1959.

Mother to ten wonderful children, grandmother to nineteen and great grandmother to one.

I live on a smallholding in Ireland with my husband Peter and youngest daughter, Fleur, four dogs, two cats, five donkeys and numerous chickens.

Thank you for reading The Tracings Of My Shadow.

The following poems included in this book *"The Tracings Of My Shadow"* were previously published online on the Write Out Loud website:

Breathless, A Hot Evening in August, Hope Ain't Gonna Float, You Held Me With Your Tears, Ripped Away, Mortality, Strength, Mask, Solitude, An Acorn's Story, The Book, Too Short for Shorts, Smile, Whispers, Who Said That, Man Is The Beast, Cooking Up A Storm.

All copyright remains the property of the author.

Table of Contents

Printed in Great Britain
by Amazon